ABOUT
DAMS

By Mabel Harmer
Illustrated with photographs

Melmont Publishers, Inc.
Chicago, Illinois

To John Gregory Spencer whose dams will not always
be built in sand

Library of Congress Catalog Card Number 63-7003

The author's thanks go to H. E. Siminson, Director
of Information, Bureau of Reclamation, Salt Lake City, Utah,
who reviewed her manuscript for accuracy of detail.

Photographs courtesy of the United States Bureau of Reclamation

TABLE OF CONTENTS

Farm land saved by irrigation

WHY MAN BUILDS DAMS

Have you ever seen a dam? Perhaps you have made one of sticks and mud across a small stream. A dam is something built to hold back running water.

Dams are built for many reasons. One very important reason is to save water to be used in time of need.

A lot of water falls every year. Millions of gallons for each one of us comes down as rain, hail, or snow. That ought to be enough. So it might be if the moisture came down in the same amounts in all parts of the country. But it doesn't. Some places get more than is needed while others get too little. Dams help make the best possible use of all the water that falls.

We use more and more water all the time. Large cities, such as New York and Los Angeles, use enormous amounts. Seventy-five years ago only a few homes had bathtubs. Now almost every home has one or more.

Besides, there are a great many more people in the United States than there were seventy-five years ago.

Farmers use more and more water all the time. When there are several dry years, a drought sets in. Dust storms blow away the good topsoil. Irrigation is the only thing that can save the farm land, and irrigation means **water**.

Dams store water to make electricity. Electricity turns the machinery that manufactures almost everything we use. Electricity lights our homes. Mother uses it to run her washing machine. It heats the iron with which she irons our clothes. Many stoves for cooking food use electricity.

Dams are also built for flood control. All across the country dams now hold back the rivers that once could destroy thousands of farms and homes, as well as the lives of people and animals.

Dams are among the biggest things man builds today. The Grand Coulee Dam in the state of Washington is bigger than the Empire State Building in New York City or the pyramids of Egypt.

Orchard dying from lack of water

CHOOSING THE DAM SITE

Dams must be built where they will be safe for the people who live downstream from them.

Many years ago people tried to build dams out of the branches of trees and bushes, logs and rocks. These dams were much like those built by beavers. Such a dam would hold well enough with an ordinary run of water. But what if there were a cloudburst? The crude dam would be the first thing to go. A raging flood would roar down the river bringing with it driftwood, haystacks, and even animals. It would wash away fields, homes, and other buildings.

The big dams today are built to last. For that matter, so are the smaller ones. No amount of time, money, and effort is too much to make sure they will last.

The first problem is to choose the best possible site for the dam. Many questions have to be answered. Where will the dam serve the greatest number of people? Is the site fairly near the materials that will be needed to build the dam? Above all, is the site a safe one on which to build?

Surveying for a dam site

Much of this work is done by surveyors and engineers. Sometimes they study and plan for years before they find the answers to these questions. When Hoover Dam was being planned, several sites were studied before Black Canyon was selected. It was chosen because it was very narrow. The rock walls were considered strong enough to support the weight of the dam and the reservoir waters.

Surveying the site can be a dangerous, breathtaking job. Men have to go down the jagged sides of the mountain by means of ropes and hooks to help decide in which direction the dam will be built.

Dam sites are often a long way from the source of the necessary building materials. Usually roads have to be built so materials can be gotten to the site before work can begin on the dam. In Arizona 112 miles of new road had to be laid to the site of Roosevelt Dam.

Railroad tracks must at times be laid in order to haul rocks, gravel, and other heavy materials to the site. Nearly twenty-three miles of track were needed for Hoover Dam.

The site of Glen Canyon Dam on the Colorado River was far from both roads and towns. It is only 1,000 feet from one rim of the canyon to the other at the dam site. However, before a steel bridge was built near the spot, trucks were traveling 200 miles to bring supplies from one side of the canyon to the other.

Page, Arizona, near Glen Canyon Dam

Usually a town must also be built near the site for the workers and their families.

Dragline being loaded

Giant carry-all

12

Next the site has to be cleared for the dam itself and for the lake and reservoir that will hold the water. Men bring in heavy machines to do this work.

A giant carry-all with twenty elephant-power opens its enormous jaws and — GULP! Up come six tons of dirt at a single bite.

The dragline picks up tons of boulders and dirt, then dumps them into a hopper where they are separated.

There is an entire farmyard parade of machinery. Bulldozers rumble along moving dirt and gravel. Next come the cats — the caterpillar tractors. They can move almost anything, including other machinery. Sheepsfoot rollers trample down the dirt.

Bulldozer at site of Navaho Dam

There are big jobs for both men and machinery. Before Shasta Dam was built in California, part of a railroad had to be moved. Thirty miles of new track, eight bridges, and twelve tunnels were built.

Railroad tracks also had to be moved for Boysen Dam in Wyoming. This time a tunnel was built under the dam abutment. Now a train travels beneath the water for more than a mile.

New York City draws its water supply from more than 1,000 rivers, lakes, small streams, and wells. Large amounts of water come from four rivers — the Croton, the Bronyx-Byram, the Catskill, and the Upper Delaware. To get all this water called for the building of many dams. For just one of the dams, several bridges, highways, and fourteen cemeteries had to be moved.

Tunnel near Boysen Dam

Train entering tunnel under Boysen Dam

The site of Hungry Horse Dam in Montana held still another problem. It was dense forest land with thousands of trees to be cleared away. The site was cleared with the aid of a big, steel ball fastened to the end of a wire cable. The ball, dragged by a tractor, mowed down a forest as easily as if it were a field of wheat.

Indians have always liked to live along the banks of rivers where fish and game were plentiful. In South Dakota nearly 3,000 Indians had to find new homes because of the building of a dam. Indians have had fishing rights along the Columbia River for nearly one hundred years. Now the best fishing holes are covered up by reservoirs.

Steel ball used to mow down trees

American Falls Dam

The Indians from a nearby reservation also had to move when the American Falls Dam was to be built. Their chief, Tea Pokribo, was invited to speak when the cornerstone of the dam was laid. He came dressed in colorful robes.

"In giving up this land," he said, "we are sharing with you our limited supply of bread. We needed this land to supply our humble needs. Our simple life is based on the land.

"No one not a member of our tribe can understand what this sacrifice means to us. We give it up because we want to live in peace and harmony with our white brother. We want to improve our farms and homes on the land that is left. We are trying to adapt our ways to your ways."

Sometimes an entire town has to be moved. Otherwise it would be at the bottom of the lake or reservoir. Although they have been well paid for them, many people do not want to leave their homes. In the Tennessee Valley people were living on farms that had belonged to their grandparents. They dreaded giving up this land.

Only one landmark is left of what was once the city of American Falls, Idaho. A high, white grain elevator stands in the middle of the dam's reservoir.

GETTING RID OF THE RIVER

After the site for the dam has been chosen and the land has been cleared, the next task facing the engineers is to get rid of the river. When the river is deep, wide, and swift this can be a big problem.

Before Hoover and Glen Canyon dams could be built along the Colorado River, huge tunnels were blasted through the mountains. The river was sent through these tunnels to join the main stream below. This was done so the men could work on a dry river bed.

It was no easy matter to change the course of a river that was roaring along at the speed of a freight train, but it had to be done.

Diversion tunnel at site of Glen Canyon Dam

A temporary dam, called a cofferdam, was built above the dam site just below the opening of the tunnel. This forced the river out of its bed and into the tunnel.

Another cofferdam was built below the dam site at the downstream opening of the tunnel. This was to direct the stream back into the river again.

Flume at Flaming Gorge dam site

If the river is not too wild or swift moving, the engineers may use another method. At the site of the Grand Coulee Dam on the Columbia River, cofferdams were built to block off first one part of the river then another part. The dam was built in sections.

When the stream to be dammed is a small one, the river can be gotten out of the way by sending it through pipes or an open trough called a flume.

PREPARING THE RIVER BED

After the river is out of the way, workers dig down to bedrock. This means they clear away every bit of mud and fine rock, called silt, until they reach the bottom of the river bed.

The cracks and crannies of the bed are then filled with cement, after which it is polished as smooth as if it were a giant tooth. It may take as long as two years just to prepare the river bed before the actual work of building the dam can begin.

If the dam is being built in a narrow canyon, as many dams are, the sides of the canyon must be cleared. Every loose slab or rock must be blasted away. Unless the sides of the canyon are smooth and clear, rocks may come crashing down on the workmen below.

The men who scrape the rock from the canyon walls are called high-scalers. They are lowered from the rim above in rope slings. With bars, hammers, and explosives they work from the top of the canyon walls all the way to the bottom.

The high-scaler may dangle several hundred feet above the river day after day. From a distance he looks like a puppet on a string.

After the loose rock is cleared away, the cracks are sealed with cement. Otherwise water might seep in, freeze, and widen the cracks.

PLACING THE CONCRETE

The biggest job is placing the concrete for the dam. A checkerboard of wooden boxes, called forms, rises where the dam is to stand. A single form may be as large as a good-sized house. The forms are supported by steel trestles.

Miles and miles of pipe are run through the forms and buried in concrete. As the concrete goes into the forms from giant buckets, cold water is sent through the pipes. This is done so the concrete will cool in days instead of years. Also, unless it cools quickly, the concrete will expand as it cools and sets and the dam will break. In very hot climates ice water is used.

There must be no air spaces whatever in the dam. So, after the concrete has cooled, the pipes are filled with grout — a mixture of water and cement.

When the concrete has hardened, the wooden forms are removed but the steel trestles remain. The great checkerboard squares of concrete are joined by filling the cracks with grout to make the whole structure perfectly solid.

Placing the concrete for Glen Canyon Dam

Riggers at site of Hoover Dam

THE RIGGER

Millions of pounds of steel go into a big, concrete dam. Besides the girders there are the penstocks, the huge pipes that carry the water from the reservoir into the powerhouse. These penstocks may be thirty feet in diameter. There are also outlet pipes to carry the water from the reservoir through the dam onto the spillway. The spillway is the section on the face of the dam over which water is released when the water level in the reservoir reaches a certain height.

Riggers in mid-air

A rigger is on the job to help guide the steel girders into place. Like an eagle he perches on a giant crane that swings steel wherever it is needed. He rides over the dam at a height of several hundred feet, held up by a single cable.

He learns to move about the steel girders like a squirrel, but never for one moment can he let his attention wander. A single false step and he may plunge to his death. A wrong signal from someone directing the work may also cause an accident.

Although the final ride is just as risky as the first one, it is never quite as hard.

One rigger says, "The first ride is like going into battle for the first time. Your fingers begin to shake. Your mouth goes dry. At every creak of the cable you hang on for dear life. You look down. You know the river is only 600 feet below but it looks a million miles away. Little ant-like figures are moving along the shore. They aren't ants at all. You know that well enough. Some of them are giant machines.

"Finally you get down again. Your fingers are shaking like crazy. But you are happy and excited. You feel as if you had just gone into outer space for the first time."

Some high-scalers and riggers stay on the job year after year. They are men who thrill to the challenge of danger. They know, too, that they are doing a job that needs to be done. Without their daring, the high dams could never be built.

High scalers drilling holes in a canyon wall

THE DAM RISES

As the dam rises, the job calls for many other workmen. There are welders who join the pieces of pipe that make the huge penstocks. Electricians do the wiring for the corridors and the control system.

In many dams the powerhouse is an important part of the setup. Water flows through the penstocks to the turbines which act as giant water wheels. They provide the power for the generators which create the electricity.

There may be one or more galleries, or hallways, inside the dam. These are always reinforced with steel. The galleries are used to take care of any drainage — water that might seep into the dam. They also allow for inspection by the workers and can be used for visitors who enjoy seeing the interior workings of a huge dam.

There are usually elevators to serve the galleries. The elevators at Hoover Dam drop a distance equal to forty stories.

Shasta Dam in process of construction

Shasta Lake (reservoir) behind Shasta Dam

A dam gradually narrows as it rises. Hoover Dam, for instance, is the width of two average city blocks at the base but only thirty-five feet wide at the top. A roadway is built across the top of most dams.

Behind every dam is the reservoir which is very often a good-sized lake. Because the water is held here to be released at will, it cannot tear down the river bed and cause floods. Instead, it is stored until it is needed for use in cities and on farms.

The lake and the land immediately surrounding it make a wonderful place for camping and for boating and fishing. It also serves as a refuge for water fowl and wild animals.

Lake Mead (reservoir) behind Hoover Dam

Shasta Dam spillway

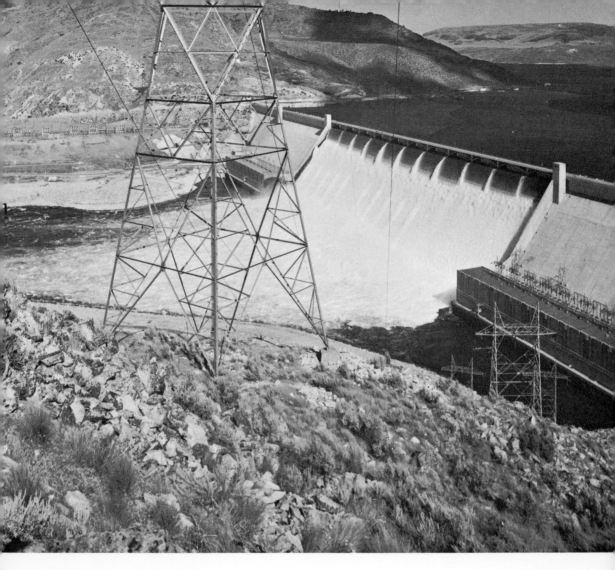

Grand Coulee Dam spillway

On the downstream side of the dam is the spillway over which the water flows when it has reached a certain height in the reservoir or when some water needs to be released. If there is a heavy rainfall and a flood might be expected, greater amounts of water can be released.

Palisades Dam, Idaho

EARTH DAMS

Not all dams are built of concrete. Two very large ones, Palisades Dam in Idaho and Trinity Dam in California, are earth dams.

The so-called earth dam is built of a mixture of gravel, sand, and rocks — all selected very carefully. Some concrete is also used, especially where it is needed to help make the dam leak proof.

The earth dam is built in places where the bedrock might not be strong enough to support a concrete dam. Another reason for deciding upon an earth rather than a concrete dam may be that the sand, gravel, and rocks are close at hand. Also, an earth dam might be the better choice in an open valley where the dam would be long rather than high.

DAMS MUST BE SAFE

Whether it is built of earth or concrete, a dam must be safe. Engineers spend vast sums of money to make sure of that. They must protect the lives of the people living near the dam.

In spite of the best efforts of the engineers, some dams have given way. As late as 1959 a dam burst in France. Mappasett Dam was a graceful arch 200 feet high. Behind it was a lake six miles long and two miles wide. The builders boasted that it was the thinnest dam in the world. Unluckily that was all too true. Five days of heavy rains swelled the lake waters. One night the dam burst wide open. The waters rushed down through the valley with such force that a train was derailed. Two hundred and sixty people died in the flood.

In 1928 the St. Francis Dam in California gave way. You may have read about the San Andreas Fault along the west coast which has been the cause of many earthquakes. The fault caused some water leakage at St. Francis Dam. Cracks appeared in the dam but they were not thought to be serious. One black night, however, the dam gave way. A hundred foot wall of water swept down the canyon. Thousands of acres of rich farm land were ruined. With them went many homes and a loss of nearly 400 human lives.

St. Francis Dam after its collapse

The worst break in this country came back in 1889. It caused the frightful Johnstown flood in Pennsylvania. The dam on the South Fork Reservoir had shown signs of cracking for some time. In spite of complaints, the lake waters were kept at a high level. Fishing and hunting were better that way. Heavy rains brought the lake to still higher levels. Finally the dam burst and the flood waters roared into the city below. Property damage was great but worse still was the loss of 2,000 lives.

The engineers who work on dams today use the greatest of care. Workmanship and materials must be of the very best quality. The seams where the steel pipes have been welded together are gone over with an X-ray machine. Any defects in these joints must be detected. The builders want to be sure that tragedies such as those just described will never happen again.

X-raying penstocks at Hoover Dam

43

THE BIG THREE

There are three giants among American dams. They are Grand Coulee, Hoover, and Shasta. Glen Canyon Dam is almost as large.

The great Hoover Dam, on the boundary between Nevada and Arizona, was built back in the 1930's. Until then the Colorado River appeared to be of no use whatever to mankind. Fish could not live in its muddy waters. There was no way to use it for irrigation. In fact it seemed bent on destruction. Time and time again, at flood stage, it washed away valuable farm land and farm crops.

At one time the river broke loose and almost destroyed the great Imperial Valley in Southern California.

Looking downstream from Hoover Dam

The only way to stop this destruction was to build a dam. Most people said it couldn't be done. They just couldn't believe there was any way to tame that raging, red river, the Colorado. The engineers said it **had** to be done so they got busy and found a way to do the impossible.

Hoover Dam rises to a towering 726 feet. The white concrete arc in the black chasm is a thing of great beauty. But it is more than a beautiful picture, it is one of the most stupendous engineering jobs that has ever been attempted.

Three other dams help Hoover Dam make a more useful river out of the Colorado. They are Glen Canyon in Arizona, Flaming Gorge in Utah, and Navaho in New Mexico.

Looking downstream at Glen Canyon damsite

Navaho Dam in process of construction   Flaming Gorge Dam in process of construction

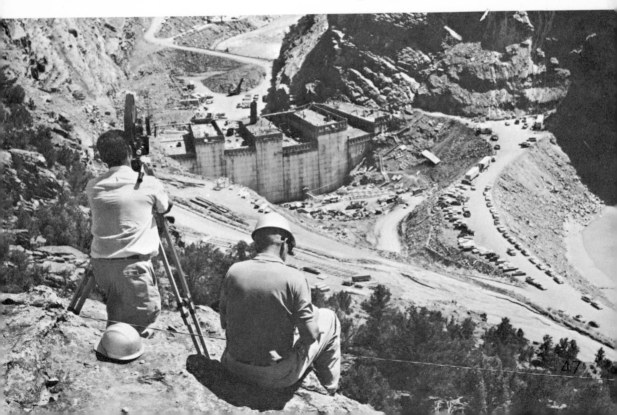

47

The Grand Coulee Dam in the state of Washington gets its name from a great natural reservoir. A coulee is a deep, narrow valley. It is almost a huge trench. This one was made by Mother Nature during the ice age. A dam of ice forced the Columbia River out of its usual course causing it to cut this deep trench. After the ice had melted, the river went back to its old bed leaving the coulee high and dry.

The coulee is so high above the river that no one ever thought of using it to store water. No one, that is, except a few dreamers whom other folk nicknamed the pumpers.

These so-called pumpers said, "Suppose the coulee could be sealed at both ends. Suppose a dam could be built across the Columbia River. Then water could be pumped up into the coulee, water that could be used to irrigate our dry and dusty farms."

Grand Coulee Dam

It took a long time to make other people believe that this could be done. The pumpers fought their battle for many years. Finally they won out and the Grand Coulee Dam was built. Behind the dam is Lake Franklin D. Roosevelt. It stretches all the way to the Canadian border, a total of 151 miles.

During World War II most of the electrical power obtained from the Grand Coulee Dam was used for ship building. More exciting, perhaps, is the fact that the heart of the atom bomb was manufactured in Hanford, a town near the Columbia River. This had been made possible only because of the huge amounts of water and power to be had from the Grand Coulee Dam.

Power house, Grand Coulee Dam

The water problem in California can be explained in a few simple words. There is too much water in the northern part of the state and too little water in the southern part. Terrible floods have occurred in the north. One in Yuba City, a few years ago, took more than forty lives and destroyed many fine homes and orchards.

The building of dams has helped to stop these floods. Water can now be stored and sent to the thirsty farms and orchards of Southern California. People in the cities are also sure of getting enough water for their needs.

The dams, pumps, and canals necessary to send this water from the north to the south form a great system. The greatest single feature of the system is Shasta Dam high in the Cascade Mountains twelve miles north of Redding.

Shasta Dam

Every dam site has its problems. At Shasta it was the thousands of acres of manzanita and poison oak that had to be cleared to make way for the huge construction plants. Another 30,000 acres had to be cleared for the reservoir. This took two years of hard work.

Shasta Dam is a very beautiful structure. Rising to a height of 602 feet, it is two thirds of a mile wide at its crest. The waterfall on the face of the dam is three times as high as Niagara Falls.

Behind the dam lies Shasta Lake, California's largest man-made lake. It is used for boating, fishing, swimming, and camping.

Up in the Sierra Nevada Mountains, east of the city of Fresno, is Friant Dam. Friant and Shasta, with the smaller dams, the canals, and waterways in between, stand guard against either the droughts or the ·floods that have destroyed so many California crops and damaged so much property in the past.

Shasta Dam

SMALL DAMS

When the pioneers first came west they found the land bone dry in many places. Sometimes it was so hard it even broke the plows. The men soon discovered there wasn't enough rainfall for the crops. Some way had to be found to bring water to the parched earth.

The settlers dug ditches leading from the rivers and the springs to their fields. So as to make sure there would always be water for the ditches, they built small dams to hold back the water. In that way the melting snows of winter could be saved for use during the dry summer months.

The men who built these dams had no concrete. They had no heavy machinery. They had only axes and shovels and their bare hands. For materials they used whatever was near by — rocks, dirt, logs, and brush.

Surprisingly enough some of these dams lasted for years. One in Utah, built over one-hundred years ago, is still in use. Of course there were other dams that went down with the first heavy spring rains. Often the farmlands near the river banks were flooded when a dam burst.

While nearly all large dams are built on rivers, this need not be the case with the small dam. Sometimes there is a natural depression, or low spot, that can be filled with water from the rain or snow in the hills above it. Or a reservoir may be fed from a number of small streams or even from springs. Of course there must be a barrier, a dam, to hold back the water.

Small dams are usually placed rather close to the territory they are to serve. That is the chief reason why they should be so well built as to be completely safe. They, as well as the big dams, must be built on foundations of solid bedrock. They may be built either of concrete or earth.

These small, community dams are very important. Their reservoirs supply the water for lawns and gardens and nearby farms. They fill the hoses for the local fire department. People depend upon the reservoirs for the water they use in their homes. Sometimes the water stored by the dam is used to create electrical power for the surrounding towns.

Deer Creek Dam and power plant, Provo Canyon, Utah

Many small dams have been built to help out the bigger ones. Along the Tennessee River, for example, there are several such dams that hold back the water in the mountains until it is needed to fill up big brother dam.

There are big dams and little dams all over our country and many more continue to be built. Even so, men have not been able to keep up with the ever increasing need for more and more water. Many large cities are in constant danger of having the supply run low. There have been times in New York City when it was against the law to have a leaky kitchen faucet.

Since there is about the same amount of water on the earth now as there was in the beginning, new ways have to be discovered for making better use of the water already on hand.

Scientists have been trying for quite some time to change sea water into fresh water by removing the salt. Ways have been found to do this. There are even plants in which it is already being done. But the processes still cost too much so men keep on looking for ways to get the salt out of the water more cheaply. Some day they will be successful. In the meantime we can be grateful to the far-seeing men who have given us our wonderful system of dams.

Salt water conversion plant at Freeport, Texas

INDEX